Charlie

Written by Amy Algie
Illustrated by Mark Guthrie

PEARSON

Miss Lavender
did not like birds.
She did not like
their beady little eyes.
She did not like
their sharp beaks and claws.

Miss Lavender's classroom had a fish and a guinea pig, but it did not have a bird... until Charlie came.

One day, the kids
were reading their books.
Miss Lavender was reading
with a group.
Then she looked up.
"Who is whistling?" she asked.
No one said anything.

Miss Lavender went back
to her group.

I'm a pretty boy.
Give me a kiss.
Give me a kiss.

Miss Lavender looked
around the class.
"Who said that?" she asked.

The kids began to laugh.
Then Miss Lavender turned around.
She saw the bird.
"Oh, no!" she said.

The bird fluffed up its feathers.
It looked at Miss Lavender
with its beady eyes.
"My name's Charlie," it said.
"My name's Charlie.
Give me a kiss.
Give me a kiss."

The kids laughed,
but Miss Lavender didn't.

Miss Lavender flapped her hands at Charlie.
"Get out of here," she said.

Charlie flew into the air.
He flew around and around.
The kids chased Charlie around the room.

Charlie flew to Miss Lavender.
He landed on her shoulder.
"Give me a kiss," he said.
Miss Lavender screamed.

Then the principal came in.
"What is all this noise?" she asked.

Charlie flew to the principal.
He landed on her head.
"Give me a kiss," he said.

The kids laughed.
The principal laughed.
Then Miss Lavender laughed, too.

The principal took Charlie
in her hands.
"Someone will be looking
for you," she said.

The kids made a sign.
They put it outside the school.

Charlie's owner came to get him.
"Silly boy, Charlie," he said.

"Give me a kiss," said Charlie,
and everyone laughed.

Found Sign

Found

Grey cockatiel.
His name is Charlie.
He likes to say,
"Give me a kiss."
Come to Room 5 to
pick him up.

◼◤ Guide Notes

Title: Charlie

Stage: Green Bridging Orange

Genre: Fiction

Approach: Guided Reading

Processes: Thinking Critically, Exploring Language, Processing Information

Written and Visual Focus: Found Sign

Word Count: 279

THINKING CRITICALLY

(sample questions)

- What do you think this story could be about?
- Look at pages 2 and 3. Why do you think Miss Lavender didn't like birds? What might have made her think this way?
- Look at pages 6 and 7. How do you think Miss Lavender felt when the kids laughed and she didn't?
- Look at pages 10 and 11. Why do you think Miss Lavender laughed, too, when Charlie landed on the principal's head?
- Look at page 13. How do you think making a "found sign" will help Charlie?
- Look at page 14. How do you think the owner felt when he came to get Charlie?

EXPLORING LANGUAGE

Terminology

Title, cover, illustrations, author, illustrator, title page

Vocabulary

Interest words: beady, guinea pig, whistling, principal
High-frequency words (new): their, until, everyone, someone
Compound words: classroom, anything, someone

Print Conventions

Capital letter for sentence beginnings and names (**M**iss **L**avender, **C**harlie); full stops, ellipsis, exclamation marks, question marks, quotation marks, commas, apostrophes